God's Projected Plan To Stop Terrorism

Life of Abraham Revisited God Blessed Isaac and Ishmael Role of Jesus Christ Highlighted

God's Projected Plan To Stop Terrorism

Moses A Talabi

Published by Moses Talabi, 2021.

While every precaution has been taken in the preparation of this book, the publisher assumes no responsibility for errors or omissions, or for damages resulting from the use of the information contained herein.

GOD'S PROJECTED PLAN TO STOP TERRORISM

First edition. April 17, 2021.

Copyright © 2021 Moses A Talabi.

ISBN: 978-0999252147

Written by Moses A Talabi.

This book is dedicated to the Lord God and to the expansion of the kingdom of God in the world.

The book is dedicated to the reign of peace and love in the world, as contained in the intents of God for his kingdom.

The book is dedicated to all the peoples of the world who share the view that terrorism must stop in the world.

MOSES TALABI

ISBN 978-0-9992521-4-7 (Paperback)

ISBN 978-0-9992521-5-4 (Digital)

Original Edition Copyright © 2017 by Moses Talabi under the title: The Origin of Terrorism and God's Plans for Extermination.

Revised Edition Copyright 2020 by Moses Talabi under the title: God's Projected Plan To Stop Terrorism

All rights reserved. No part of this publication may be reproduced, distributed, or transmitted in any form or by any means, including photocopying, recording, or other electronic or mechanical methods without the prior written permission of the publisher.

All scripture quotations are taken from the King James Version of the Bible, unless otherwise stated.

Printed in the United States of America. This book is a publication of

Jesus' Legacies Ministry International, Inc. Email: jesuslegacies@gmail.com

CONTENTS

Introduction 5

Chapter One 8
The Origin of Terrorism

Chapter Two 25
The World Today

Chapter Three 30
A Summary of the Crux of the Matter

Chapter Four 36
The Church of Jesus and the Gates of Hell The Passion of Jesus for the Arab Nations

Chapter Five 38
Way Out of Terrorism

Chapter Six 43
Rulers of Nations, God's Endowed Partners

Chapter Seven 48
God's Endowments start with salvation

Addendum 50

About the Author 62

DEDICATION

This book is dedicated to the Lord God and to the expansion of the kingdom of God in the world.

The book is dedicated to the reign of peace and love in the world, as contained in the intents of God for his kingdom.

The book is dedicated to all the peoples of the world who share the view that terrorism must stop in the world.

INTRODUCTION

Terrorism: Prosperity of Peoples' Knowledge of God Required

At a critical point in the lives of the Jews, God raised up Zechariah as a prophet; and Zechariah declared as written:

> "Cry yet, saying, Thus saith the LORD of hosts; My cities through prosperity shall yet be spread abroad; and the LORD shall yet comfort Zion, and shall yet choose Jerusalem" --- Zechariah 1:17.

Not Necessarily Financial Prosperity

In the above quoted Word, God says prosperity shall be the instrument to spread His cities to all over the world.

What is prosperity in the context of the subject matter in this book; is it financial? No; it is knowledge. Knowledge is an asset—a great asset.

Knowledge is a great asset in the store of God designed by God to spread His cities to all over the world. In other words, knowledge of God shall prosper, understanding of God shall prosper; and through knowledge of God, and understanding of Him, the cities of God shall spread to all over the world.

Secondly, what are the reasons for God to demand the spread of His cities to all over the world? The reasons are numerous.

But the primary, most important reason is to enhance the expansion of God's Kingdom of peace and love in the world.

Particularly, knowledge and understanding of God and His acts is designed by God for the spread of His cities among the nations of the generational descendants of Ishmael and the nations of the generational descendants of Isaac; especially those of these two different descendants whose activities necessitate the subject matter of this book.

Jesus came to put the Word of God in Zechariah 1:17 into effect in the lives of the peoples of the nations of the descendants of Isaac, the Jews; and alike, in the lives of the peoples of the nations of the descendants of Ishmael, the Arabs.

Abraham, by God's grace, is a vital figure in the plan of God for the expansion of His Kingdom upon earth; and Isaac and Ishmael are sons of Abraham.

When we tell the story of the life of Abraham we cannot omit Ishmael and Isaac.

When we give the account of the ministry of Jesus Christ we cannot omit any part of the entire world. A great message of the Kingdom of God Jesus brought to earth is that peace and love must reign in the world.

The world must wake up to peace.

The Jews nations, the Arab nations, the other nations of the world must wake up to peace. God is waiting on them all concerning the works of commitment to peace.

Not Human Idea of Terrorism

This book is about a matter with spiritual origin.

It is not about world or regional uprisings that are political, social, or economic.

The subject matter of this book does not relate to dictionary or academic meaning of Terrorism. The subject matter relates to divine revelation; because it is a matter from above.

"He that cometh from above is above all" John 3:31

The subject matter is not earthly in origin; rather, it is heavenly; but the effect of the matter weighs heavily upon the earth.

Commitment to the resolution of this matter is earthly—earthly by the peoples' understanding and knowledge of God; and reflecting that knowledge and understanding in their approach to the resolution of the matter; because this matter has nagged the earth for long and subjected the world to a hassle.

When the peoples of the world commit themselves to the resolution of this matter, they will receive the back-up from the heavenly places.

For, the truth stands that:

"The earth is the LORD'S, and the fulness thereof; the world, and they that dwell therein." --

--Psalm 24:1

So, the subject matter of this book is not about the human idea of terrorism.

A world subjected to a hassle

For a considerably long time, the world has been subjected to a hassle, searching for answer to the bitter experiences of terrorism.

A large part of the peoples of the world are aware that terrorism is largely connected with religion—that terrorism is hinged on a spiritual source.

But the world has failed to explore the reason why religion is connected with terrorism; so as to pin- point the exact source.

Knowing the exact source will probably prompt the addition of salt to this source where bitter experiences emerge.

Speaking frankly, the source is known.

The source is known because there are glaring Words in the Bible which point to the exact source of terrorism. There is no idle Word in the Bible.

Also, there is no occurrence in this world which does not have the clue in the Bible.

There is no issue of life which the Bible does not explicitly address; yea, not about a matter which is as serious as terrorism!

So, the exact source of the bitter experiences of terrorism is known-- as revealed inside this book.

Attention to the source of this bitter experiences is the matter that is inadequate.

This book therefore draws the attention of all the peoples of all the nations of the world to the Word of the Lord, as written:

"Then saith he unto his disciples, The harvest truly is plenteous, but the labourers are few; Pray ye therefore the Lord of the harvest, that he will send forth labourers into his harvest" Matthew 9:37—38.

In this connection, this book also admonishes all the peoples of all the nations of the world to live in consciousness of the divine information inscribed on the outside of the back cover of this book concerning terrorism; that the unpleasant incidents of terrorism may end in the world.

Arguments and Counter Arguments about Terrorism

As discussed inside this book, terrorism is basically a matter between the generational descendants of Ishmael and the generational descendants of Isaac – the two sons of Abraham. All along, arguments and counter arguments have been made, one side accusing the other of being the terrorist.

And each side has supporters among the nations of the world – from the East, from the West. But Jesus, Whom the Bible describes as the Wisdom of God, stands in the middle of the two sides cum supporters, and cries:

> "Does not wisdom cry? and understanding put forth her voice? She crieth at the gates, at the entry of the city, at the coming in at the doors. Unto you, O men, I call; and my voice is to the sons of man. Hear; for I will speak of excellent things; and the opening of my lips shall be right things. By me kings reign, and princes decree justice. The LORD possessed me in the beginning of his way, before his works of old. Then I was by him, as one brought up with him: and I was daily his delight, rejoicing always before him; Rejoicing in the habitable part of his earth; and my delights were with the sons of men. Now therefore hearken unto me, O ye children: for blessed are they that keep my ways."
>
> -----Proverbs 8:1, 3, 4, 6, 15, 22, 30, 31, 32.

Jesus says the LORD—God the Father—possessed Him in the beginning of the Father's way, before His works of creation of the earth.

Jesus says He is rejoicing in the habitable part of the earth; that is, the world where the peoples live. And He says His delights are in the peoples of the world.

The Epistle to the Colossians emphasizes the role of Jesus Christ more vividly, as written:

> "For by him were all things created, that are in heaven, and that are in earth, visible and invisible, whether they be thrones, or dominions, or principalities, or powers: all things were created by him, and for him; And he is before all things, and by him all things consist."
>
> ------Colossians 1:16—17.

Already, God the Father had sent Jesus to the world.

And Jesus had brought the Kingdom of God to the world, in authentication of His delights which are in the peoples of the world, as written in Proverbs 8:31 quoted above.

Chapter one
The Origin of Terrorism

Terrorism in the world originated inadvertently from the family of Abraham, a notable friend and servant of God. Terrorism negates the intent of God for the world into which His Kingdom has come. Therefore, the content of this book can be seen as highlighting a paramount project of God pre-designed by God for execution at the due time. The due time is the New Testament ministry era of Jesus Christ, which is the era in which the Kingdom of God is established in the world. It is also the era of atonement of sins of all the peoples of the earth without any exception; apart from the several other benefits of the ministry of Jesus Christ for the enhancement of good life.

But, why the emphasis on "without any exception"? This is so because terrorism is in the world today due to lack of understanding of God and His acts by some categories of peoples; and these categories of peoples need to know that Jesus came to the world partly because of them. So, "without any exception" is meant to emphasize their inclusion in the programs of Jesus Christ for the world. Therefore, this book is particularly directed to the attention of these categories of peoples, as well as to the whole world.

What need to be understood by the relevant categories of peoples

It is a long story which the world knows about; but we need to refresh our minds about the story, though concisely.

God had created man – Adam -- in His own image. But Satan engaged the mind of Eve, Adam's wife, and deceived her to eat the forbidden fruit. Adam succumbed to Eve's engaged mind, ate the forbidden fruit and thereby incurred God's curse; although, the curse was not directly on Adam or Eve; but God cursed the ground for Adam's sake –Genesis3:17.

After that, God projected the New Testament ministration era of Jesus Christ, so that Jesus would accomplish God's programs in the world in lieu of Adam due to Adam's failure.

Hence, the Bible refers to Jesus as the last Adam –1 Corinthians 15:45.

God started this New Testament ministration era of Jesus Christ by calling Abraham as the beginning point – Genesis 12:1.

So, Abraham may be referred to as the springboard for the world to jump into the New Testament era of Jesus Christ.

But here again, Sarah, Abraham's wife, being oblivious of God's plan, gave her maid Hagar to Abraham to be his wife and bear children for the family due to her barrenness. Abraham too succumbed to Sarah's oblivious mind, took Hagar as his wife and got a son Ishmael by her in

a scheme which was not devised by Hagar herself; and she was not in any way involved in the planning of the scheme.

Certainly, God was not pleased with the scheme; and part of the tone of Genesis 16:7—16 quoted below is a pointer to God's displeasure. God was not pleased because the actions of

Abraham and Sarah, at that initial time of their walk with God, amounted to another destabilization of His planned Kingdom upon earth, after Adam and Eve had caused the first destabilization. Even if Abraham did what he did in his family according to the tradition of his time in his nation, the call on him by God had made him a divinely separated man, away from tradition, and for God's use --- Genesis 12:2-3.

God says: "My people are destroyed for lack of knowledge" – Hosea 4:6.

So, lack of knowledge of God at that initial time of Abraham's walk with God hindered him from focusing on God Who had told him: "And I will make of thee a great nation, and I will bless thee, and make thy name great, and thou shalt be a blessing." Genesis 12:2.

Any scheme embarked upon by a person or family, that is not God's plan will not work; rather, the unexpected may result.

Eventually, confusion set into Abraham's new polygamous family as Sarah and Hagar became enemies; and Hagar was forced out of the family into the wilderness.

God, the Omnipotent, Omnipresent, and Omniscient saw all that happened.

God's displeasure made manifest

So, the story continues as written below, wherein God's displeasure was made manifest: "And the angel of the LORD found her by a fountain of water in the wilderness, by the

fountain in the way to Shur. And he said, Hagar, Sarai's maid, whence camest thou? and

wither wilt thou go? And she said, I flee from the face of my mistress Sarai. And the angel of the LORD said unto her, Return to thy mistress and submit thyself under her hands. And the angel of the LORD said unto her, I will multiply thy seed exceedingly, that it shall not be numbered for multitude.

And the angel of the LORD said unto her, Behold, thou art with child, and shalt bear a son, and shalt call his name Ishmael; because the LORD has heard thy affliction. And he will be a wild man; his hand will be against every man, and every man's hand against him; and he shall dwell in the presence of all his brethren. And she called the name of the LORD that spake unto her, Thou God seest me: for she said, Have I also here looked after him that seest me? Wherefore the well was called Beerlahai-roi; behold, it is between Kadesh and Bered. And Hagar bare Abram a son: and Abram called his son's name, which Hagar bare, Ishmael. And Abram was four score and six years old, when Hagar bare Ishmael to Abram. --- Genesis 16:7—16.

The above quoted Word of God may appear ordinary; but it is not. The Word has a far- reaching effect on world affairs today.

The Word is like a fulcrum on which the lever of world security turns.

Put simply, the Word is the springboard of terrorism in the world. It is so because, Abraham by God's grace, stands out as a very significant factor in the plans of God for His Kingdom in the world through Jesus Christ. And Abraham, being the springboard of this New Testament era, an error committed by him due to his initial lack of knowledge of God's acts resulted in serious consequences, the major one of which is the precipitation of terrorism.

By God's grace, Abraham had a long walk with God; and all along, God continually renewed his mind.

Jesus Christ the Son of God, came to the world in the flesh, as a human being, through the loins of Abraham, according to God's predetermined counsel.

Can the world not realize that the above quoted Word partly carries an expression of God's displeasure? There is no Word of God in the Bible that amounts to an idle Word. Every Word is intended to accomplish a definite purpose that must be accomplished.

The only One God has appointed to modify His Word is His Son Jesus Who has come to the world to establish the Kingdom of God and put in place arrangements for the expansion of the Kingdom.

And if the world realizes that the above quoted Word carries an expression of God's displeasure, should the world not make determined efforts to explore the role of Jesus Christ in the resolution of the problem of terrorism, knowing fully well that Jesus came to re-align all human beings to God?

If anyone is in doubt

In case there is anyone or any group of people that are in doubt of what I have stated about the effect of the Word of the angel of God to Hagar, I invite the people to think and reflect on the effect of the Word spoken to Adam in Genesis.

God told Adam:

"cursed is the ground for thy sake. Thorns also and thistles shall it bring forth to thee."

-----Genesis 3:17—18.

This Word of God to Adam may appear ordinary; but it is not.

Several categories of catastrophic occurrences that have occurred in the world, which make people uncomfortable, just as thorns and thistles make people uncomfortable, are related to this Word.

These catastrophic occurrences have come in diverse dimensions, some of which the world may not be able to properly decipher.

The Epistle to the Romans makes it more explicit to us as written:

> "For the earnest expectation of the creature waiteh for the manifestation of the sons of God. For the creature was made subject to vanity, not willingly, but by reason of him who hath subjected the same in hope, Because the creature itself also shall be delivered from the bondage of corruption into the glorious liberty of the children of God." ------ Romans 8:19 21

What is the creature in the above quoted Word?

All created non-living things—inanimate things-- particularly the ground, constitute the creature.

Who subjected the creature to vanity and bondage of corruption? God did; when He told Adam:

"cursed is the ground for thy sake. Thorns also and thistles shall it bring forth to thee"

-----Genesis 3:17--18

So, we should not take the Word spoken to Hagar lightly; in the same way that we do not take the Word spoken to Adam lightly.

However, Romans 8:19—21 quoted above says God subjected the creature to vanity and bondage of corruption in hope – in hope of better times when the Kingdom of God would have come to the earth with the glorious benefits—as expounded partly below in this chapter, and partly under further chapters of this book. Essentially, in hope of better times when God's original intention for the world would have been restored— when there shall be no terrorism in the world; because the Kingdom of God relates to the whole world without any exception.

The Full Revelations to be received from Romans 8:19--21

During the process when God was executing His pre-determined counsel to bring the Kingdom of God to the world, God involved two people, first Adam and then Abraham.

But each of them destabilized God's plans in two different ways.

The two different destabilizations have been identified and detailed earlier in this book. The reactions of God to the two different destabilizations have also been identified and detailed.

God, being merciful, enacted His reactions in hope for all the peoples of the world—in hope of the time when His Son Jesus would bring the Kingdom of God to the world.

That is, all the Words spoken at those initial times—to Adam about the ground—and to Hagar about Ishmael—which were Words of negative effects, were all spoken in hope of later better times for the peoples of the world.

The later better times are the New Testament ministry times when the Kingdom of God would have come to the world.

God expects some works on the part of all the peoples of the nations of the world in order to realize this hope.

Because faith without works is dead; hope without adequate works to match is wishful thinking.

And later in this book, it is pointed out that both the generational descendants of Isaac and the generational descendants of Ishmael are to be partakers of this realized hope.

My Intention

My intention in this book is not to cast aspersions on, or show contempt to, any portion of the generational descendants of Ishmael; rather, the book is intended to draw their attention to the plan of God for all human beings in the Kingdom of God.

My intention in this book is not to cast aspersions on, or show contempt to, any portion of the generational descendants of Isaac; rather, the book is intended to draw their attention to the plan of God for all human beings in the Kingdom of God.

The book is also not intended to compare religion; it is not to compare Christianity with Islam, or, vice versa.

The book has nothing to do with an appraisal of any religion.

The book is simply drawing attention to the various Words of God in the Bible as they relate to peace and love in the world; and the things God requires of the peoples of the nations of the world in order that peace may reign.

Primarily, the focus of the book is the need to stop terrorism in the world.

The God signified in the Bible

The Bible records God's Word, as written"

> "Remember the former things of old: for I am God, and there is none else; I am God, and there is none like me, Declaring the end from the beginning, and from ancient times the things that are not yet done, saying, My counsel shall stand, and I will do all my pleasure." saiah 46:9—10

The Bible also records God's Word, as written:

> "Who is he that overcometh the world, but he that believeth that Jesus is the Son of God? This is he that came by water and blood, even Jesus Christ; not by water only, but by water and blood. And it is the Spirit that beareth witness, because the Spirit is truth. For there are three that bear record in heaven, the Father, the Word, and the Holy Ghost: and these three are one." 1 John 5:5—7

This second quoted Word signifies God as One; made up of the Father, the Word, and the Holy Ghost.

In the gospel according to St. John, chapter 1, verses 1—5, the Bible signifies Jesus as the Word. And a presentation of One God signified in the Bible is made, as written:

> "Go ye therefore, and teach all nations, baptizing them in the name of the Father, and of the Son, and of the Holy Ghost" Matthew 28:19

The Foundation

The sum total of the above quoted various Words about the God signified in the Bible is the foundation upon which this book is written.

All that are written above indicate that the Bible emphasizes the prevalence of God the Father, God the Son Jesus, and God the Holy Ghost-- presented as the Holy Trinity.

Suffice it to state the following four points:

1. Various Bible Words emphasize that the principle of the service rendered to the God of heaven and earth, rather than to the God of this world, is built on the belief in the prevalence of the Trinity; that is, God the Father, God the Son Jesus, and God the Holy Spirit.
2. A great number of millions of Christian believers all over the world have shared evidences and practical life experiences that establish belief in the prevalence of the Trinity; that is, God the Father, God the Son Jesus, and God the Holy Spirit.
3. When a religious individual believes in the prevalence of this Trinity, that individual will also be convinced that there is only One God manifested as the Father, the Son, the Holy Spirit.
4. If any number of different religious organizations have different beliefs and convictions about God, they do not serve the same God.

However, it is up to everyone concerned to choose what religion to embrace; there is absolutely no enforcement of choice involved.

Most importantly, the God signified in the Bible does not impose force on anyone concerning who to serve; but He admonishes all the peoples of the world to come to Him through His Son Jesus Christ.

What need to be Understood Continues

As far as Jesus is concerned, the description of Ishmael in Genesis 16:7—16 quoted earlier does not fit into the Kingdom He brought to the world.

He came not to condemn or discredit anyone; but to save all the peoples of the world and bring them into the Kingdom of God together in peace and love.

Jesus would not cherish the descendants of Ishmael being associated with that description, because it negates the intent of the Kingdom of God which He brought to the world.

Jesus plunged the description out of the way. And Jesus is not alone in that intent.

He says:

"And he that sent me is with me: the Father hath not left me alone; for I do always those things that please him"---John 8:29.

So, as will be seen later in this book, part of the role of Jesus Christ was that He reversed the description and made it invalid in the lives of all the generational descendants of Ishmael that accept and believe in Jesus Christ.

Why the Word spoken about Ishmael triggers Terrorism

God's Word says:

> "For as the rain cometh down, and the snow from heaven, and returneth not thither, but watereth the earth, and maketh it bring forth and bud, that it may give seed to the sower, and bread to the eater: So shall my word be that goeth forth out of my mouth: it shall not return unto me void, but it shall accomplish that which I please, and it shall prosper in the thing whereto I sent it." saiah 55:10 - 11.

According to the above quoted Word, God says His Word shall accomplish that which He please; His Word shall prosper in the thing He sent the Word; and the Word shall accomplish the purpose for which He sent it.

Evidently, the Word which God sent through His angel to Hagar for the description of Ishmael in Genesis 16:7 - 16 quoted earlier was not a complimentary Word; rather, it was a contrary Word; although the Word must be accomplished.

The reason for this contrary Word about Ishmael is as follows:

Before God called Abraham, God had concluded His plans for the structure of Abraham's family. The structure is as written:

> "But my covenant will I establish with Isaac, which Sarah shall bear unto thee at this set time in the next year" Genesis 17:21

God said so because He had mapped out a covenant that would run from Abraham to Isaac; and to Jacob; for the execution of His plan - which culminated in the advent of Jesus Christ in the world.

But before God made that plan known to Abraham, he and his wife Sarah, had unilaterally devised the plan for Abraham's family by taking Hagar as his wife to bear children for the family due to Sarah's barrenness.

God was not pleased with that plan made by Abraham; because God viewed the plan as an act of the destabilization of His own plan.

And God saw Ishmael as the offspring of the act of the destabilization of His plan. God showed His displeasure by pronouncing that contrary Word on Ishmael.

That was in the same way God cursed the ground for Adam's sake because God was not pleased with what Adam did; and God pronounced thorns and thistles as the products of the ground - which give discomfort.

Likewise, the contrary Word which God pronounced on Ishmael depicted an attitude that engenders terrorism and counter terrorism - a situation that results in severe consequences, and severe discomfort on every side concerned.

The Word was neither due to the fault of Ishmael, nor due to the fault of Hagar. Isaac was not even born at that time; so, the Word was not due to his fault either.

But the after- effects of the contrary Word weigh heavily on both the generational descendants of Ishmael and the generational descendants of Isaac.

The Word was entirely due to the error of the lack of understanding of God's acts by patriarch Abraham at that initial time of his walk with God.

What concerns the world now is to learn from the Word in the search for peace to replace terrorism.

Patriarch Abraham had his mind continually renewed by the Words of God; Abraham's life was a testimony of continual obedience to the Words of God; and Abraham walked with God for a considerable length of time.

Let us all also yield our minds to God; that the Words of God may renew us - Romans 12:2 - that we may emulate patriarch Abraham; that terrorism may come to an end in the world.

More importantly also, our merciful God enacted His reactions both to Adam and to Abraham in hope for all the peoples of the world; as indicated earlier in this chapter under the sub-title: The Full Revelations to be received from Romans 8:19 - 21.

Therefore, there is no need for anyone or any people to be worried or troubled; or angry. There is no need for anyone or any group of people to continue in acts of terrorism; or commit any act that is akin to terrorism; or execute any action that amounts to terrorism in disguise.

The life of Ishmael as relayed in the Bible portrayed one of the land- mark events that took place in the world while God was setting this divine stage called the Kingdom of God.

Jesus had set the stage for the world to be at ease and in peace; waiting for all the peoples of the world to come to God through Him, as demanded by God the Father.

Let all the peoples of the world come to God through Jesus Christ.

Let all the peoples live at ease and in peace; as they commit themselves to diligence in works and productions that cater for the people's needs and welfare.

Let all the peoples of all the nations of the world commit themselves to taking practical steps that will actualize that glorious hope which is in Jesus Christ.

Jesus came to take care of whatever is contrary to any one or any people that accept Him, as written:

> "Blotting out the handwriting of ordinances that was against us, which was contrary to us, and took it out of the way, nailing it to his cross." -—Colossians 2:14.

Therefore, in order that the world may not continue to grapple with terrorism, it will be highly glorious if the world puts up a collective effort to accept Jesus. It may look impossible; but all things are possible to them that believe –Mark 9:23. God will not bend or break His Word to suit the world. God has magnified His Word above all His name –Psalm 138:2. A scripture cannot be broken—John 10:35. God will not change - Malachi 3:6; it is the peoples that will change; and adjust to God's Words; because God built the nature of change into human beings.

Revelations from Isaiah 55:10 - 11

Human beings constitute the only segment in all of God's creations to whom the Words of God are directed.

The purpose of this is that human beings will receive the Words, ponder and meditate on them; and engage the Words for fulfilment of the Words' desired purposes.

Prophet Jeremiah had insight into this divine phenomenon; and said unto God:

"Thy words were found, and I did eat them; and thy word was unto me the joy and rejoicing of mine heart: for I am called by thy name, O LORD God of hosts"

------Jeremiah 15:16

Several and larger segments of human beings in all nations of the world receiving similar insights from the Words of God is the way for peace and termination of terrorism in the world. The world experiences One God Whom the Bible describes as the Creator of all things, including human beings.

Can any human being have pre-eminence over the God that created him; so that this human being will consider himself higher than God's Words? God will not allow that.

<u>At the time the angel of God spoke about Ishmael, the Kingdom of God was in the heavenly places, even prior to the Old Testament ministration times operated by Moses.</u>

These times that were prior to the Old Testament were the times of Adam and Abraham, when sin was in the world; but sin was not imputed because there was no law-- Romans 5:13.

In that wise, the Old Testament can be described as extracting it's beginning from the initial times, so that the Old Testament law could expose sin---which was what the Old Testament actually did Romans 7:7 - 13.

The Bible describes the Old Testament as the ministration of condemnation, and the New Testament as the ministration of righteousness.

The Bible then declares as written:

"For if the ministration of condemnation be glory, much more doth the ministration of righteousness exceed in glory. For even that which was made glorious had no glory in this respect, by reason of the glory that excelleth. For if that which is done away was glorious, much more that which remaineth is glorious." 2 Corinthians 3:9 - 11

Concerning the generational descendants of Ishmael that accept Jesus Christ, their placement in the Kingdom of God is governed by the above quoted Word. Their placement is wrapped in the ministration of Jesus which exceeds much more in glory than any ministration before it.

Now, Jesus has brought the Kingdom of God into the world in His New Testament – New Covenant Ministration, with the New Testament Word.

The generational descendants of Ishmael are required to receive that New Testament Word into their mind, to replace the Old Word spoken by the angel of God.

The generational descendants of Ishmael need to have an understanding of God in this matter.

And then Jesus declared:

> "And this gospel of the kingdom shall be preached in all the world for a witness unto all nations; and then shall the end come." Matthew 24:14

Terrorism shall first come to an end in the world in which we live now; by reason of the preaching of the Gospel of the Kingdom.

The end relating to God's intent in this quoted Word shall come according to God's determinate counsel and time.

The intentions of Jesus—righteous intentions—are focused on all the nations of the world. The generational descendants of Ishmael need to commit themselves to the New Testament, New Covenant Word which Jesus came to establish.

By doing that, they are committing themselves to the God of their generational father, Abraham.

Speaking by the Spirit, Apostle Paul says:

> "Blessed be the God and Father of our Lord Jesus Christ, who hath blessed us with all spiritual blessings in heavenly places in Christ" Ephesians 1:3.

Apostle Paul was raised up by the God of Abraham, the generational father of the descendants of Ishmael.

Apostle Paul is attesting to the truth that the Kingdom of God which was in the heavenly places has now been brought down to us on earth by Jesus Christ.

The blessings spoken about by Paul are provided under the Kingdom of God which Jesus brought to the world.

Appropriating the blessings need commitment to the Kingdom of God and the New Testament, New Covenant Word.

The Word spoken by the angel of God about Ishmael cannot be broken; because no scripture can be broken (John 10:35); it cannot be annulled; but it can be replaced with the New Testament, New Covenant Word.

As long as the generational descendants of Ishmael do not fill their minds with the New Testament Word, the Old Word of the angel of God will prevail, direct their lives, and remain as the trigger for terrorism; or in some cases, terrorism in disguise; because that Word, being the Word of God, it cannot be broken, it cannot be annulled; it can only be replaced by the New Testament, New Covenant Word.

The New Word for the Generational Descendants of Ishmael

Concerning the generational descendants of Ishmael that accept Jesus, the new description God gives them presents the role of Jesus in their lives as follows:

> "Blotting out the handwriting of ordinances that was against us, which was contrary to us, and took it out of the way, nailing it to his cross." Colossians 2:14.

Jesus cancelled the description, took the handwriting of the description out of the way, and nailed it to His cross.

The nations of the generational descendants of Ishmael, the Arab nations, need to key into the Kingdom of God, because the Kingdom of God is the Kingdom of their generational father, Abraham; and the Kingdom relates to all the nations of the earth without any exception.

That is one of the reasons the Bible says:

> "For God so loved the world, that he gave his only begotten Son, that whosoever believeth in him should not perish, but have everlasting life. For God sent not his Son into the world to condemn the world; but that the world through him might be saved." -

> --------John 3:16 - 17

That is the way to end terrorism in the world.

The conflict between the Arabs and the Jews due to different religious beliefs is the wing on which terrorism flies; even though patriarch Abraham ties them together in the flesh; and even though God paved the way for a change to spiritual tie over two thousand years ago.

Also, when terrorists operate, they destroy not only people of the opposite faith, but in many cases, they destroy themselves also, which is a striking irony of religious belief.

For the sake of terminating Terrorism

But, for the sake of terrorism to come to a stop, the Arab nations coming up with a national policy to promote the expansion of God's Kingdom in the world, thereby serving the God of their generational father Abraham, will be a policy well pleasing to God.

In this connection, we will revert to the Word about Jesus Christ under the introduction of this book:

The Epistle to the Colossians emphasizes the role of Jesus Christ more vividly, as written:

> "For by him were all things created, that are in heaven, and that are in earth, visible and invisible, whether they be thrones, or dominions, or principalities, or powers: all things were created by him, and for him; And he is before all things, and by him all things consist." Colossians 1:16 - 17.

Added to this is the Epistle to the Ephesians, as written:

> "And to make all men see what is the fellowship of the mystery, which from the beginning of the world hath been hid in God, who created all things by Jesus Christ:" ----

> --------Ephesians 3:9

The Word just quoted says God the Father used Jesus to create all things. The Gospel according to St. John which introduces Jesus as the Word also says:

> "All things were made by him; and without him was not anything made that was made". John 1:3

The above three Words attest that Jesus made all things: the world, all things physical and non- physical, animate including human beings and all inanimate.

Can anything made have pre-eminence over the One that made it?

Colossians 1:16 - 17 quoted above says all things were created by him, and for him.

Human beings, particularly, were created for Him so that He can take them along; that they may serve God through Him for the expansion of the Kingdom of God which He brought to the world.

The peoples of the Jewish nations are enjoined to make themselves available to 'walk with God' in this assignment of Jesus Christ.

The peoples of the Arab nations are enjoined to make themselves available to 'walk with God' in the assignment.

Patriarch Abraham, the generational father of the generational descendants of Isaac and Ishmael walked with God for a long time.

The two sides of the generational descendants of Abraham should do the same; and thereby, bring terrorism to an end.

Dichotomy of Faith Practitioners

Meanwhile, a dichotomy of faith practitioners has emerged from the generational descendants of Abraham.

Is this dichotomy of faith God's plan for the world; seeing that the peoples' faith is intended to be focused on the Kingdom of God; and seeing that the Kingdom of God came to the world through the loins of Abraham, the father of Isaac and Ishmael?

Very striking is the truth that several dimensions of each of the dichotomy have also emerged, all operating under different facets; some resulting in destruction of lives and property.

And some operations result in the killing of self.

Killing of self occurs due to lack of understanding of the works of God through Jesus Christ. Herein lies the need for the Arab nations to fully explore the role of Jesus Christ in the world; that the killing of self and other people may stop.

Does destruction of self or other people fit into God's intension for creating the earth?

Does enmity between the human portion of God's creations align with God's plan for creating the earth?

Do the human portion of God's creations - the peoples - glorify God by acts of destruction? These are pertinent questions the entire world must address; and provide answers to God, the Creator of all things.

The culture of "It does not concern me" does not provide the genuine answer to the God of Abraham, the father of Ishmael and Isaac; the God Who created all things.

That culture of "It does not concern me" must be got rid of; because the culture does not glorify God.

The matter on ground does concern everyone in the world; because, commitment to the expansion of the Kingdom of God is the answer to diverse manners of uncomfortable occurrences, manifesting not only as terrorism, but also as some unfathomable incidents.

Abraham's Family and God's Continuous Guide

The gifts and calling of God are without repentance. God would not change His mind on what He had called Abraham to do in His kingdom. God would only perfect all things concerning Abraham and the world. That is one of the reasons Jesus came to the world.

The world has taken the simplicity in the Word of God—the simplicity that is in Christ-- as a matter to simply gloss over. It should not be so.

The entire peoples of the world should properly meditate on God's Word quoted earlier from Genesis 16:7 - 16.

They should also meditate on the various Words relating to the ministry of Jesus Christ. There is no idle Word in the written Words of God in the Bible.

Every Word is sent to accomplish a definite purpose. God says:

> "For as the rain cometh down, and the snow from heaven, and returneth not thither, but watereth the earth, and maketh it bring forth and bud, that it may give seed to the sower, and bread to the eater: So shall my word be that goeth forth out of my mouth: it shall not return unto me void, but it shall accomplish that which I please, and it shall prosper in the thing whereto I sent it." saiah 55:10 - 11.

God's Word is not wasted; it must serve the intended purpose. However, where a Word has been modified due to the advent of Jesus Christ with His New Testament ministration, the relevant New Testament Word prevails.

For example, all curses under the Old Testament have been cancelled under the New Testament, as written:

> "Christ hath redeemed us from the curse of the law, being made a curse for us: for it is written, Cursed is every one that hangeth on a tree: That the blessing of Abraham might come on the Gentiles through Jesus Christ; that we might receive the promise of the Spirit through faith." Galatians 3:13 - 14.

All the curses that were in place by reason of the Old Testament laws administered by Moses had been cancelled by Jesus Christ in the behalf of all the peoples of the world that accept Him and believe in Him.

Likewise, as has been emphasized earlier in this chapter, all the Words of God's displeasure concerning the birth of Ishmael have been cancelled by the various Words of the ministry of Jesus Christ for the whole world.

Who are the descendants of Abraham

After Ishmael was born, the story on Abraham's family continues as written:

"And when Abram was ninety years old and nine, the LORD appeared to Abram, and said unto him, I am the Almighty God; walk before me, and be thou perfect.

Neither shall thy name any more be called Abram, but thy name shall be Abraham; for a father of many nations have I made thee. And God said unto Abraham, As for Sarai thy wife, thou shalt not call her name Sarai, but Sarah shall her name be. And I will bless her, and give thee also a son of her: yea, I will bless her, and she shall be a mother of nations; kings of people shall be of her. And Abraham said unto God, O that Ishmael might live before thee! And God said, Sarah thy wife shall bear thee a son indeed; and thou shalt call his name Isaac: and I will establish my covenant with him for an everlasting covenant, and with his seed after him. And as for Ishmael, I have heard thee: Behold, I have blessed him, and will make him fruitful, and will multiply him exceedingly; twelve princes shall he beget, and I will make him a great nation. But my covenant will I establish with Isaac, which Sarah shall bear unto thee at this set time in the next year."

-----Genesis 17:1,5,15,16,18,19,20,21

"And the LORD visited Sarah as he had said, and the LORD did unto Sarah as he had spoken. For Sarah conceived, and bare Abraham a son in his old age, at the set time of which God had spoken to him. And Abraham called the name of his son that was born unto him, whom Sarah bare unto him, Isaac. And Sarah saw the son of Hagar the Egyptian, which she had born unto Abraham, mocking. Genesis 21:1 - 3, 9.

The last sentence in the above quoted Word says Sarah saw the son of Hagar, Ishmael, mocking. The scripture continues by saying that Sarah prevailed on Abraham to send Hagar and her son Ishmael out of the house. God stepped in and told Abraham to hearken to what Sarah told him.

So, Abraham sent Hagar and her son Ishmael out of the house into the wilderness of Beersheba.

Speaking about Ishmael, the Word of God continues as written:

"And God was with the lad; and he grew, and dwelt in the wilderness, and became an archer. And he dwelt in the wilderness of Paran: and his mother took him a wife out of the land of Egypt." Genesis 21:20 - 21.

From all that are written above, the descendants of Abraham are the descendants of Isaac and the descendants of Ishmael.

Both Isaac and Ishmael have their own descendants, which in the present-day context have become several generational descendants.

All the generational descendants of Isaac and Ishmael put together form the generational descendants of Abraham.

Chapter two

The World Today

The present-day world is witnessing a bitter war between some generational descendants of Isaac and some generational descendants of Ishmael, all of which form the generational descendants of Abraham. The bitter war has resulted in terrible acts of terrorism with diverse destructions of lives and property.

Ishmael's Descendants and Knowledge of God

Under the introduction of this book I wrote the following:
   Particularly, knowledge and understanding of God and His acts is designed by God for the spread of His cities among the nations of the generational descendants of Ishmael and the nations of the generational descendants of Isaac; especially those of these two different descendants whose activities necessitate the subject matter of this book.
   Jesus came to put the Word of God in Zechariah 1:17 into effect in the lives of the peoples of the nations of the descendants of Isaac, the Jews; and alike, in the lives of the peoples of the nations of the descendants of Ishmael, the Arabs.
   An important thing being emphasized is that the generational descendants of Ishmael should not allow anything to hinder them from seeking the knowledge of the God of their generational father, Abraham.
   Some of the vital points which the terrorists have not recognized and put into practical use are as follows:

1. Even though God was not pleased with the scheme by which Sarah gave Hagar to Abraham to be his wife as shown in Genesis 16:7 - 16, the love which God demonstrated to Hagar and Ishmael is manifest in the same Word. God is love.

This love is a component of the fruit of the Spirit which is embedded in the Kingdom of God. This is the love passed on to us, being receivers and beneficiaries of the Kingdom of God.
   And it is the love God has established to cement together the descendants of Isaac and the descendants of Ishmael.
   It is this kind of love that should permeate their relationship and bind them together.
   God knows all things ahead of time. God knew that the Kingdom of God would come to the earth.
   This love of God is what should engage the minds of the various generational descendants of Isaac and Ishmael.
   This love of God is what all of them should propagate and manifest to one another.
   But rather, hatred has engaged their minds due to lack of understanding of God and His acts; and that hatred is what they demonstrate to one another.

God cares. God manifests care borne out of love. God's care is epitomized and heightened by the advent of Jesus Christ into the world as shown more vividly further down in this book.

1. The whole scenario contains a portion which should be deeply meditated upon in order to understand it; to avoid hostility between the descendants of Isaac and the descendants of Ishmael.

The portion is as written below:

"Now we, brethren, as Isaac was, are the children of promise. But as then he that was born after the flesh persecuted him that was born after the Spirit, even so it is now.

Nevertheless what saith the scripture? Cast out the bondwoman and her son: for the son of the bondwoman shall not be heir with the son of the freewoman. So then, brethren, we are not children of the bondwoman, but of the free." Galatians 4:28 - 31

The above quoted Word serves two purposes.
First, the Word reviews the incident between Sarah, Hagar and Ishmael at the initial times, the times which had been relegated to mere initial records; and have no relevance to our present New Testament dispensations.
Jesus came to the world to forestall any confusion which that initial Word might generate; in that the provision of the Kingdom of God He brought to the world emphasizes that 'there is neither bond nor free' as stated below in Galatians 3:27 - 29.
Secondly, the last sentence of the Word quoted in Galatians 4:28 - 31 above points out that born again Christians are brethren, that is, brothers and sisters.
The brothers and sisters are made up of people that originate from the generational descendants of Isaac who have accepted Jesus; and people that originate from the generational descendants of Ishmael who have accepted Jesus Christ.
And that is quite apart from the fact that in the New Testament era of Jesus Christ, there is neither bond nor free, as written:

"For as many of you as have been baptized into Christ have put on Christ. There is neither Jew nor Creek, there is neither bond nor free, there is neither male nor female: for ye are all one in Christ Jesus. And if ye be Christ's, then are ye Abraham's seed, and heirs according to the promise." Galatians 3:27 - 29

Equal Spiritual Genealogical Relationship

By virtue of all that are written so far under this subsection, Jesus came to establish equal spiritual genealogical relationship to Abraham for those who accept Him from the generational descendants of Isaac; and for those who accept Him from the generational descendants of Ishmael.
That is part of the intents of the Kingdom of God; thereby enhancing a situation that forbids terrorism from any side.

Will some generational descendants of Ishmael deny Abraham as their generational father? God for-bid.

What might have happened along all the ages does not annul the truth that Abraham is the father of Ishmael.

None of the supporters of one side or the other can annul the truth that Abraham is the father of Ishmael and Isaac.

All the various peoples concerned are enjoined to give peace a chance.

All are enjoined to embrace the Kingdom of God which has come to the world through the loins of Abraham; whether from Isaac's side or from Ishmael's side, or from the supporters' side.

By that, the benefits of the Kingdom of God which Jesus brought to the world will be appropriated by all the generational descendants of Abraham.

Let all the peoples get committed to the expansion of the Kingdom of God. That is the answer to terrorism in the world.

1. God blessed Isaac and Ishmael and provided for each of them as written below:

"And as for Ishmael, I have heard thee: Behold, I have blessed him, and will make him fruitful, and will multiply him exceedingly; twelve princes shall he beget, and I will make him a great nation. But my covenant will I establish with Isaac, which Sarah shall bear unto thee at this set time in the next year." Genesis 17:20 - 21

Further Words of God reveal that the covenant which God promised to establish with Isaac is the New Testament ministration Covenant of Jesus Christ, which is the era of the Kingdom of God in the world; the Kingdom which Adam could have established in the world but failed due to sin.

This covenant is designed to bring all the peoples of the world together in peace and love, inclusive of all the generational descendants of Isaac and Ishmael.

The covenant is designed to bring all the peoples of the world together in worship of God through Jesus Christ.

The covenant is further authenticated by the prophecy of the psalmist which says:

"All nations whom thou hast made shall come and worship before thee, O Lord; and shall glorify thy name."
Psalm 86:9.

In the Word of God quoted from Genesis 17:20 - 21, God told Abraham that He would make Ishmael a great nation.

And indeed, Ishmael has become a great nation, the nation of the Arabs!

Will members of the nation God made from Ishmael not fulfill the Word written in Psalm 86:9 just quoted by coming to worship before the God of their generational father Abraham?

Will God be pleased if the people fail to glorify His name as demanded in the Psalm? Will engagement in terrorism glorify God and His name?

Besides, if God made Ishmael a great nation, does that nation not belong to God just in the same way as the nation made from Isaac belong to God?

Several Biblical Words reiterate emphatically that no one can approach that God of Abraham except through Jesus Christ.

And the God which the Bible portrays is the God of Abraham. That is the God Who created all things including all human beings.

1. In Genesis chapter 18, the Bible narrates the incident of the visit of three angels of God to Abraham during which the angels revealed the news of the birth of Isaac to Abraham.

The testimony of God concerning Abraham on this occasion is highly illuminating. The testimony is as follows:

"And the LORD said, Shall I hide from Abraham that thing which I do; Seeing that Abraham shall surely become a great and mighty nation, and all the nations of the earth shall be blessed in him?" Genesis 18:17 - 18

The LORD says all the nations of the earth shall be blessed in Abraham.

That is, the great nation which God promised to make Ishmael in Genesis 17:20 - 21 quoted earlier is one of the nations of the earth which shall be blessed in Abraham.

In another scripture, God's Word also says:

"Now to Abraham and his seed were the promises made. He saith not, And to seeds, as of many; but as of one, And to thy seed, which is Christ." Galatians 3:16

The above Word says that all the promises of God to Abraham are projected to come into effect through Jesus Christ. The entire world which God says shall be blessed in Abraham are to receive the blessings through Jesus Christ.

The two sons of Abraham, Isaac and Ishmael, and their generational descendants are to receive the blessings God promised Abraham through Jesus Christ.

What further illumination do the warring descendants of Isaac and Ishmael need? Here again, the question arises:

Will the generational descendants of Ishmael deny that Abraham was the father of Ishmael? Will the Christian world deny that Abraham was the father of Ishmael?

1. The Bible reveals a very significant role of Jesus Christ in the lives of the entire peoples of the world, as written:

"For verily he took not on him the nature of angels; but he took on him the seed of Abraham." Hebrews 2:16

Jesus took on Him the nature of human beings, the inhabitants of all the nations of the earth which God had promised to be blessed in Abraham, as written in Genesis 18:17—18 quoted earlier.

Jesus took on Him the nature of human beings who have all fallen due to the fall of the first man, Adam; and as a result of the fall, human beings suffer due to the activities of Satan who masterminded the fall and continues to oppress the peoples of the world in various dimensions. Jesus did not take on Him the nature of angels who had fallen due to the fall of arch angel Lucifer – Isaiah 14:12.

Rather, Jesus chose to come to the earth as a human being, so that He too would partake of the sufferings of all human beings – which He did on the cross; and suffered for all the peoples of the world.

The Bible continues this glorious role of Jesus Christ, as written:

> "Wherefore in all things it behoved him to be made like unto his brethren, that he might be a merciful and faithful high priest in things pertaining to God, to make reconciliation for the sins of all the people." Hebrews 2:17

What are we saying?

Jesus came to embrace all the peoples of the earth as His brethren, be their merciful and faithful high priest.

Jesus suffered on the cross for the whole peoples of the world in order that He might reconcile all the peoples to God in whatever sins or errors they have committed – even sins or errors committed by their generational parents and generational ancestors.

And having done all that, Jesus declared: "It is finished" John 19:30

Chapter three

A Summary of the Crux of the Matter

Jesus already came to the world. God sent His Son Jesus to perfect all things that concern the entire human race. God, Who has the divine ability to see the future, saw all the corruption that was in place and the dangerous effects it would produce. So, God sent His Son Jesus to the world. Herein lies the crux of the matter.

Jesus came to set the world free from terrorism and other world afflictions.

How beautiful and glorious it would be for the whole world if they hear Jesus Christ and follow Him.

How wonderful it would be if the generational descendants of Isaac and Ishmael will all see the need to embrace Jesus Christ.

Jesus had a fundamental package which He came to deliver to the world.

The package is the Gospel of the Kingdom of God, to be disseminated on the platform of peace and love, and to fly on the wing of peace and love.

Love, first for God, and then for fellow human beings.

How beautiful and excellent it would be if the peoples of the nations of the world would allow the ministry of Jesus Christ, backed up by the power of the Holy Spirit Who is now resident in the world, to effect the desirable changes in the world.

God desires that all the generational descendants of Abraham have knowledge of that.

But the present- day faith practitioners predominantly operate under two camps: one operating under the camp of Isaac, and the other operating under the camp of Ishmael; and the two camps have their faith practiced in opposite directions.

Diverse dimensions of faith practitioners in each of the two camps have emerged in several different locations of the world; some camp members operating with intense extremism.

Talking about God and His works, the Bible says:

> "And hath made of one blood all nations of men for to dwell on all the face of the earth, and hath determined the times before appointed, and the bounds of their habitation."

--------Acts 17:26

The Word just quoted reiterates the truth that God made all the peoples of the earth from a common beginning, one source, one blood -- all for a common purpose which terrorism negates.

The two conflicting sides of the descendants of Abraham have not committed themselves to the Gospel of the Kingdom of God which Jesus Christ brought to the world.

As stated above, the Gospel of the Kingdom is the Gospel of peace and love ---love, first for God and then for fellow human beings.

God's Word says: "He that loveth not knoweth not God; for God is love" – 1 John 4:8

The Last Adam - 1 Corinthians 15:45

Furthermore, the plan of God can be understood by reverting to the Word which says:

> "For if by one man's offence death reigned by one; much more they which receive abundance of grace and of the gift of righteousness shall reign in life by one, Jesus Christ. Therefore as by the offence of one judgment came upon all men to condemnation; even so by the righteousness of one the free gift came upon all men unto justification of life." Romans 5:17 - 18.

The above quoted Word stands as a flash—flashing and bringing to our minds the essential works which Jesus came to the earth to do as the last Adam.

By the offence of Adam, judgment came upon all the peoples of the world to condemnation. But by the righteousness of Jesus with God the Father, the free gift of salvation came upon all the peoples of the world unto justification –for those that accept Jesus.

However, right now, some segments of the peoples of the world are in error, having allowed misunderstanding of God's works to mislead them into acts of terrorism.

They thereby engage in disobedience against God's plans just as Adam did.

Jesus came as a man in human flesh, endowed with God's grace, and clothed with righteousness as with a robe.

Jesus came with forgiveness for whatever errors the peoples of the world have committed. Jesus came to bring all peoples into righteousness with God just as He too is in righteousness with God; and into obedience to the Words of God.

Jesus came to establish peace between all the peoples of the world.

The peoples of the world need to receive revelations from the scenario presented by the Word of God quoted from Romans 5:17—18 above, in order to free themselves from terrorism.

To an ordinary mind it may look impossible. But to a mind stretched out seeking faith in God, it will be possible; for with God nothing shall be impossible—Luke 1:37.

Reconciliation of the Jews and the Gentiles

The New Testament ministry of Jesus Christ for the reconciliation of the Jews and the Gentiles as detailed in Ephesians 2:11 - 19 should attract the attention of the peoples of the world in their search for peace on earth. A very much relevant part says:

> "Wherefore remember, that ye being in time past Gentiles in the flesh, who are called Uncircumcision by that which is called the Circumcision in the flesh made by hands; But now in Christ Jesus ye who were sometimes far off are made nigh by the blood of Christ. For he is our peace, who hath made both one, and hath broken down the middle wall of partition between us; Having abolished in his flesh the enmity, even the law of commandments contained in ordinances; for to make in himself of twain one new man, so making peace; And that he might reconcile both unto God in one body by the cross, having slain the enmity thereby: And came and preached peace to you which were afar

off, and to them that were nigh. For through him we both have access by one Spirit unto the Father. Now therefore ye are no more strangers and foreigners, but fellow-citizens with the saints, and of the household of God." Ephesians 2:11, 13 - 19

From this Word of God, we see that Jesus came to abolish the law of commandments contained in ordinances that separated the Jews from the Gentiles.

By God's original design, the descendants of Jacob who was the son of Isaac, formed the nation of the Jews; and whoever is not a Jew is a Gentile.

Hence, by God's original design, the descendants of Ishmael could be deemed as belonging to the Gentile nations.

But Jesus came to destroy the separation and the enmity that existed between the Jews and the Gentiles.

Jesus came to unite the peoples from all nations, Jews or Gentiles, into one body, the body of Christ, administered by the Holy Spirit.

Hence, God's Word says:

"For as many of you as have been baptized into Christ have put on Christ. There is neither Jew nor Greek, there is neither bond nor free, there is neither male nor female: for ye are all one in Christ Jesus. And if ye be Christ's, then are ye Abraham's seed, and heirs according to the promise." Galatians 3:27 - 29.

In the Word just quoted, 'there is neither Jew nor Greek' means there is neither Jew nor Gentile.

The Word also emphasizes that all descendants of Abraham and all inheritors of God's promises to Abraham have been aligned into Jesus Christ.

Lack of understanding of God hinders the relevant peoples---the descendants of Ishmael--from seeing all the above plans of God through the ministry of Jesus Christ.

By reconciling the Jews and the Gentiles, Jesus had reconciled all the peoples of the earth as one people and one body, the body of Christ, administered by the Holy Spirit.

That is the legacy of peace bestowed by Jesus Christ for the whole world. <u>The Gospel of Total Redemption and the Descendants of Ishmael A Mystery for the Descendants of Ishmael And the Whole World</u>

According to the predetermined counsel and plan of God, the death of Jesus on the cross should not be in vain, concerning all the peoples of the earth and concerning the earth itself. When Adam disobeyed God in Genesis, God had said unto Adam:

"Because thou hast hearkened unto the voice of thy wife, and hast eaten of the tree, of which I commanded thee, saying, Thou shall not eat of it: cursed is the ground for thy sake; in sorrow shalt thou eat of it all the days of thy life; Thorns and thistles also shall it bring forth to thee; and thou shalt eat the herb of the field; In the sweat of thy face shalt thou eat bread, till thou return unto the ground; for out of it wast thou taken: for dust thou art, and unto dust shalt thou return." -—Genesis 3:17 - 19

God cursed the ground for Adam's sake due to Adam's disobedience. God pronounced thorns and thistles as Adam's harvest for his labor of tilling the ground. In addition, Adam lost the divinity—the presence of God-- that pervaded the garden of Eden where God had placed him. He was chased out of the garden of Eden into the world of corruption, vanity and hopelessness.

But Jesus came to redeem both human beings and the ground back to the original status in which they were in the garden of Eden.

So, according to God's predetermined counsel, all created things: human beings and the ground; that is, human beings and inanimate objects, are made to go through redemption under the ministry of Jesus Christ, as written:

"The Spirit itself beareth witness with our spirit, that we are the children of God: And if children, then heirs; heirs of God, and joint-heirs with Christ; if so be that we suffer with him, that we may be also glorified together. For I reckon that the sufferings of this present time are not worthy to be compared with the glory which shall be revealed in us.

For the earnest expectation of the creature waiteth for the manifestation of the sons of God. For the creature was made subject to vanity, not willingly, but by reason of him who has subjected the same in hope. Because the creature itself also shall be delivered from the bondage of corruption into the glorious liberty of the children of God."

------Romans 8:16 - 21

According to the above Word which depicts the plan of God, human beings will first escape the bondage of corruption and manifest as sons of God; and then, inanimate creature (the ground) will also be delivered from the bondage of corruption into the glorious liberty of the children of God.

Implied Revelation

The truths being revealed to us at this point is that by the manifestations of righteous lives by the peoples of the world through the ministry of Jesus Christ, the plan of God described above will be accomplished.

That is, under the ministry of Jesus Christ, human beings and all creature—human beings and the ground--- will be delivered from the bondage of corruption!

Herein lies a mystery which human beings need to understand, ponder on it, and apply it in the search for peace to replace terrorism.

It is a mystery because the Kingdom of God is wrapped in mysteries---Luke 8:10.

The peoples of the entire world need to crave for the knowledge of the mysteries of the Kingdom of God, by faith in Jesus Christ.

Only searchers through faith in Jesus Christ will know the mysteries.

Before looking into the mystery, let us explore the fuller details of the truths being revealed to us:

The Word in Romans 8:16 - 21 is revealing to us that the original plan of God at the time of creation cover all living things, the major parts of which are the human beings; and also cover all non- living things, the major part of which is the ground.

The Word is also revealing that Jesus Christ came to restore whatever the human beings lost, and whatever the ground lost due to Adam's sin.

This plan of restoration will be accomplished by righteous approach to life in general; and by righteous approach to matters that border on obedience to God's Words concerning all areas of life—to the delight of God's heart.

God is love – 1 John 4:8.

The delight of God is that His love be extended to the peoples of the world through the instrumentality of the various world governments, business corporations, churches, companies and others; for the purpose of provision of infrastructures that cater for life, righteous businesses, education, health care, and various other welfares.

God's delight is that His love be extended to the peoples by promotion of righteous marriages and family lives, where God's Word takes pre-eminence over human ideas; and by providing for the safety of the peoples' lives and properties.

The Mystery to Ponder on, and apply for Peace

The mystery to meditate upon is this:

If the ground—inanimate objects—will be delivered from the bondage of corruption into the glorious liberty of the children of God, then why should a portion of the descendants of Abraham – the descendants of Ishmael –not also be translated into the glorious liberty of the children of God?

Whereas, this glorious liberty is a blessing brought by Jesus Christ Who in the flesh, is a seed of Abraham (Galatians 3:16); and whereas, Ishmael's generations have generational fatherhood in Abraham?

Why would the whole peoples of the earth not put up a collective effort to resist whatever hinders some descendants of Ishmael from enjoying the glorious liberty of the children of God? Why would the entire peoples of the world not utilize God's prescribed method, which is the Gospel of Jesus Christ—the Gospel of peace-- to end the spirit of terrorism which hinders some descendants of Ishmael from receiving the glorious liberty of the children of God?

The Bible furthers this mystery of God by intimating us, as written:

"That in the dispensation of the fulness of times he might gather together in one all things in Christ, both which are in heaven, and which are on earth; even in him:"

------Ephesians 1:10

The above Word says God's eventual plan is to gather together all things, both which are in heaven, and which are on the earth, in Christ.

What is it that should be strong enough to exclude a portion of the descendants of Abraham – a portion of the descendants of Ishmael – from this gathering together?

Referring to the accomplishments of Jesus in the behalf of His believers, Colossians 2:14 says "Blotting out the handwriting of ordinances that was against us, which was contrary to us, and took it out of the way, nailing it to his cross"

The implied extended meaning of this Word is that Jesus had taken out of the way the handwriting of ordinances that are capable of excluding the descendants of Ishmael from the gathering together described in Ephesians 1:10 above.

So, Jesus had opened the way for the generational descendants of Ishmael to enter the Kingdom of God through Jesus Christ.

Chapter four

The Church of Jesus and the Gates of Hell The Passion of Jesus for the Arab Nations

There is a burden on my heart to draw the attention of the generational descendants of Ishmael, the Arab nations, to the subject matter of this chapter, using Apostle Peter as the reference point; as recorded in 'The Gospel According To St. Luke'.

By what is to be considered as a manifestation of the mystery of the Kingdom of God, Jesus had passion for Peter who was a fisherman, right from the first day Peter encountered Him.

And Peter immediately humbled himself to accommodate the passion Jesus had for him; and he reciprocated the passion; in that Peter too immediately developed passion for the Word of God.

The encounter is recorded as follows:

> "And it came to pass, that, as the people pressed upon him to hear the word of God, he stood by the lake of Gennesaret, And saw two ships standing by the lake: but the fishermen were gone out of them, and were washing their nets. And he entered into one of the ships, which was Simon's, and prayed him that he would thrust out a little from the land. And he sat down, and taught the people out of the ship. Now when he had left speaking, he said unto Simon, Launch out into the deep, and let down your nets for a draught. And Simon answering said unto him, Master, we have toiled all the night, and have taken nothing: nevertheless at thy word I will let down the net. And when they had this done, they inclosed a great multitude of fishes: and their net brake.
>
> ------Luke 5:1 - 6

This scripture records further that after this first encounter, Peter and his partners in the fishing business forsook all their ships; and followed Jesus.

Peter – The Church of Jesus Personified

Apostle Peter towered to a height among the disciples to the extent that Jesus declared him as the rock upon which He would build His church –signifying that the church is the people; and Peter stood out as the beginning person out of those people---Jesus made Peter the first church in the world!

Jesus had asked His disciples a question, as written:

> "But whom say ye that I am?" And Simon Peter answered and said, Thou art the Christ, the Son of the living God. And Jesus answered and said unto him, Blessed art thou, Simon Barjona: for flesh and blood hath not revealed it unto thee, but my Father which

is in heaven. And I say also unto thee, That thou art Peter, and upon this rock I will build my church; and the gates of hell shall not prevail against it. And I will give unto thee the keys of the kingdom of heaven: Matthew 16:15 - 19

Peter, being the first church in the world, Jesus gave unto him the keys of the Kingdom of heaven which Jesus brought to the world—that Peter might be the first church to enter into the Kingdom; and other churches –other peoples-- would follow suit.

Jesus, noting that the churches—the peoples-- are the inhabitants of the Kingdom of God which must expand, He declared authoritatively: "and the gates of hell shall not prevail against it".

Signifying that nothing shall be strong enough to resist anyone coming into the Kingdom of God to contribute to the expansion of the Kingdom.

Because the expansion of the Kingdom of God is in direct proportion to the expansion of the peoples of the world—peoples of all the nations of the world-- that come into the Kingdom.

So, Jesus ordained the peoples of the world as the churches that will occupy the Kingdom of God.

By that, the cities of God shall spread to all over the world as stated in Zechariah 1:17 quoted in the introduction of this book—-because the cities of God shall practically express the Kingdom of God.

Thereby, the end to terrorism in the world shall be enhanced.

God's Finger of Direction to the Arab Nations

The fore-going short narration about Peter stands as God's Finger of direction to the generational descendants of Ishmael, the Arab nations, with generational fatherhood in patriarch Abraham through whose loins Jesus came to the world.

The narration stands as expression of the passion of Jesus for the peoples of the Arab nations; just in the same way that His passion is for the peoples of the other nations of the world.

Jesus desires that the peoples of the Arab nations develop passion for the Word of God just as Peter did.

Jesus has given the key into the Kingdom of God to Peter who is a seed of patriarch Abraham through Isaac and then Jacob.

As far as the ministration of Jesus is concerned, the generational descendants of Ishmael are encouraged to come into the Kingdom of God which Jesus brought from heaven to the world. The delight of Jesus is to establish a new world order in which terrorism will be no more.

Because the delights of Jesus are with the peoples of the world – Proverbs 8:31 In that connection, Jesus gave the Great Commission, as written:

"Go ye therefore, and teach all nations, baptizing them in the name of the Father, and of the Son, and of the Holy Ghost: Teaching them to observe all things whatsoever I have commanded you: and, lo, I am with you alway, even unto the end of the world."

------Matthew 28:19 - 20

Chapter five

Way Out of Terrorism

Two avenues are available to the peoples of the world in their efforts against terrorism.

'Short- term' Measure: Human Governmental Power Application

The Word of God enjoins that we should resist the devil.

Resisting the devil includes resisting any people that yield themselves for the devil to use them for acts of terrorism due to misunderstanding of God.

Evil acts have no place to exist on earth; neither in God's laws nor in human governmental laws. The Bible says God is not willing that any should perish, but that all should come to repentance, and thereby be saved— partly signifying that no one should commit evil acts that will earn him destruction by the law of the land where he lives.

Besides, 'thou shall not kill' is a law of God, harnessed by human governments into their laws. Therefore, killing under the acts of terrorism violates the law of God and the laws of human governments.

Misunderstanding of God does not confer the right to do evil.

Human governmental weapons of resisting evil acts must be used relentlessly to resist acts of terrorism.

'Long-term' Measure: Divine Power Application

In view of all that are written so far in this book, it is evident that there is no human governmental power in this world that can finally resolve the issue of terrorism without reverting to the plan of God concerning it.

Any attempt taken, as potent, genuine, and well- meaning as it may be, will only be like a swinging pendulum which at the time of rest comes back to the starting point.

You keep on reacting it to make it swing again.

The long-term and permanent measure for the peoples of the world is to be on the Lord's side, promoting the expansion of the Kingdom of God which Jesus brought to the world; that is, to imbibe the New Testament Gospel of the Lord Jesus Christ relentlessly.

The peoples of the world need a well- planned input of global campaign for the free flow of the Gospel.

An invocation of the Gospel of peace and love in the doctrines of the Lord Jesus Christ is the way out of terrorism in the world. That is the plan of God.

The peoples of the world cannot afford to deviate from that plan.

Evidences in the Bible affirm that terrorism has spiritual undertone; that is, it is a spiritual problem. Only the divine rule power can override a spiritual problem.

There is no amount of human overriding power or lack of overriding power from the world's

Supreme Body that can terminate a spiritual problem such as terrorism.

It is a matter solely within the power of God; because God upholds all things by the Word of His power (Hebrews 1:3).

Concerning God and His Words, the Bible says:

"For thou hast magnified thy word above all thy name." Psalm 138:2.

God magnifies His Words even above His own name.

God expects the peoples of the world to magnify His Words; hold His Words in high esteem; and tremble at His Words. Concerning His Words, God says:

"So shall my word be that goeth forth out of my mouth: it shall not return unto me void, but it shall accomplish that which I please, and it shall prosper in the thing whereto I sent it." saiah 55:11.

God honors His Words; and brings them into accomplishment in and under every circumstance. Therefore, an issue that has it's beginning in God's Words can only be resolved by resorting to God's Words established for the resolution of that thing.

It is time the whole world realize that God has prerogative power over the whole world through His written Words.

The Bible emphasizes that the written Words of God control all the affairs of the entire human race.

The peoples of the world who believe that the world was created by the spoken Word of God will understand what we are talking about.

And the peoples who believe that doctrine are far in the majority!

The desire of God is that everyone shall become the righteous of God through Jesus Christ. That is the intent of John 3:17 which emphasizes that God sent not Jesus into the world to condemn the world; but that the world through Him might be saved.

By that, God's Word will be fulfilled as written:

"And all thy children shall be taught of the Lord; and great shall be the peace of thy children. In righteousness shalt thou be established: thou shalt be far from oppression; for thou shalt not fear: and from terror; for it shall not come near thee."

------Isaiah 54:13 -14.

The blessings to be derived from the above Word of God cover all areas of life.

The power for the attainment of all that are written in the Word is summarized in the Word of the Lord, as written:

"And he said, So is the kingdom of God, as if a man should cast seed into the ground; And should sleep, and rise night and day, and the seed should spring and grow up, he knoweth not how. For the earth bringeth forth fruit of herself; first the blade, then the ear, after that the full corn in the ear. But when the fruit is brought forth, immediately he putteth in the sickle, because the harvest is come." —Mark 4:26 - 29.

In accordance to the above quoted Word of the Lord, the attainment of peace in the world can be likened to the planting of food such as corn, as described in the Word. You put your seed of corn in the ground and you go to sleep and wake day and night. You come back to harvest the corn when it is brought forth. But you do not know how the seed you put in the ground became the full- grown corn you are harvesting.

Jesus says so is the kingdom of God.

That is, to harvest peace, the world needs not to hassle; but just to plant the seeds of peace, which are the Words contained in the Gospel of peace of Jesus Christ; and go to sleep and wake day and night—because in the Kingdom of God, the seed is the Word of God (Luke 8:11).

And, as stated above, the way to do that is that the world needs a well-planned input of global campaign for the free flow of the Gospel.

The world will harvest peace without knowing how the peace became full grown.

It is time the world understands that God and His ways are mysterious for those who take the steps of faith; and embark on the works of faith; and walk with God to accomplish the plans of His Kingdom.

Further on God's Plans through Jesus Christ

God desires safety and peaceful life on earth. The enemies of peace are the perpetrators of evil acts. Referring to Jesus, John the Baptist speaking by the Spirit, says:

"He must increase, but I must decrease."--- John 3:30.

Jesus' divine ideas must increase, and all human ideas must give way to His ideas, that Jesus may have pre-eminence in all things and bring about the necessary solutions to world problems.

Jesus must increase, and all evil acts must decrease.

Jesus must increase; and misunderstanding of God which gives way to satanic works must decrease.

The works of Jesus must increase, and the works of Satan must decrease. The whole affair can be likened to what we know about human politics.

Political victory derives from the outcome of the comparison of supporters' numbers. Jesus' increase and victory imply continuously greater numbers of His adherents and continuously lesser numbers of the perpetrators of evil acts.

Referring to the plans of the Almighty LORD God, the Word summaries it all, as written:

"That in the dispensation of the fullness of times he might gather together in one all things in Christ, both which are in heaven, and which are on earth; even in him."

-----Ephesians 1:10

The above Word depicts the ultimate plan of God for the whole world.

The plan of God is to gather together all human beings, all ideas, and all things, together in One -- Jesus Christ.

By that, there shall be a continuous process of increase for Jesus; and continuous decrease for satanic adherents.

Understanding the times in which we are

Concerning the present situation in the world, it will be excellent and glorious if the entire world will receive revelations from the Word of God, as written:

> "And of the children of Issachar, which were men that had understanding of the times, to know what Israel ought to do;" 1 Chronicles 12:32

The Word just quoted relates to a time when occurrences in the lives of God's chosen people in Israel were contrary to God's plans for them.

And they had to gather men and women, who had understanding of the times in which they were, to address the situation and do the necessary thing.

The Word is a highly motivating Word.

The peoples of the world need to prove that there are men and women that have understanding of the times in which we are now.

Concerning terrorism, if the Word of God does not motivate, then nothing shall be able to successfully and enduringly motivate.

That is so, because as far as this worldly realm is concerned, God upholds all things by the Word of his power. Acts of terror and destruction ravaging the world is not the plan of God for the world. It is time for the world to embrace the Gospel of peace of the Lord Jesus Christ.

The Fulness of the Gentiles

God is earnestly waiting for the execution of an assignment He committed to the already born - again Christians all over the world. The assignment is embodied in the Word of God which says:

> "For I would not, brethren, that ye should be ignorant of this mystery, lest ye should be wise in your own conceits, that blindness in part is happened to Israel, until the fulness of the Gentiles be come in. And so all Israel shall be saved: as it is written, There shall come out of Sion the Deliverer, and shall turn away unGodliness from Jacob: For this is my covenant with them, when I shall take away their sins." Romans 11:25 - 27.

God says He has kept a portion of the people of Israel in blindness so they won't see the light of Jesus and receive Him; until all the Gentiles have been brought into His kingdom in full through Jesus Christ.

Although Jesus is the Savior, the born-again Christians have the assignment to carry the Gospel of salvation to the people of Israel that have not accepted Jesus.

Today, these born-again Christians that have the assignment are made up of partly the descendants of Isaac and partly descendants of Ishmael that have accepted Jesus.

Let the already born-again Christians from the two sides work together collectively to bring the Gospel of salvation not only to the people of Israel that have not received Jesus, but more importantly, to spread the Gospel to the terrorist adherents.

In this connection, let the descendants of Isaac see the descendants of Ishmael as included factors in the Kingdom of God through Jesus Christ.

To Every Individual

If you are a born-again Christian, I pray you will continue to flow and increase in the blessings of all the highlighted Words and programs of God.

I enjoin you to do all you can do to propagate the Gospel of peace of Jesus Christ upon earth. If on the contrary you have not received Jesus into your life, I enjoin you to go ahead and receive Jesus right now; become born again; and come under the blessings of the Words and programs of God.

Above all, yield yourself to God through Jesus Christ as a tool for God's use for the expansion of God's Kingdom.

Chapter six

Rulers of Nations: Gods' Endowed Partners

God bestowed an endowment of recognition and honor on the rulers of the nations of the world in His instruction to Christian believers, as written:

> "Let every soul be subject unto the higher powers. For there is no power but of God: the powers that be are ordained of God. Whosoever therefore resisteth the power, resisteth the ordinance of God: and they that resist shall receive to themselves damnation. For rulers are not a terror to good works, but to the evil. Wilt thou then not be afraid of the power? Do that which is good, and thou shalt have praise of the same: For he is the minister of God to thee for good. But if thou do that which is evil, be afraid; for he beareth not the sword in vain: for he is the minister of God, a revenger to execute wrath upon him that doeth evil." Romans 13:1 - 4.

From this quoted Word of God, we see that God places a great premium on the rulers of the different nations of the world.

God upholds and highlights the rulers with honor, dignity and power; and He counsels Christian believers to do the same.

Indeed, God esteems the rulers of the nations of the world. Furthermore, God counseled the Christian believers, as written:

> "I exhort therefore, that, first of all, supplications, prayers, intercessions, and giving of thanks, be made for all men; For kings, and for all that are in authority; that we may lead a quiet and peaceable life in all Godliness and honesty. For this is good and acceptable in the sight of God our Saviour; Who will have all men to be saved, and to come unto the knowledge of the truth." 1 Timothy 2:1 - 4.

In the Word just quoted, God continues His esteem for the rulers of the nations of this world by asking believers in Jesus Christ to intercede and pray for them so that the outcome of their services to the people will enhance peaceful life.

God desires that the rulers serve as divine instruments of the Lord to bring the people into the knowledge of the truth of the plans of God to establish peace on earth through the Lord Jesus Christ.

And by that, the people will receive not only salvation of their souls; but will also be saved from horrible acts such as terrorism.

The total message in the two Words of God quoted establishes the truth that God recognizes the rulers of the different nations of the world as His partners in the works of the expansion of His kingdom.

Further Message to the Rulers

The Word of God disseminates the message to rulers further, as written:

"For unto whomsoever much is given, of him shall be much required" —Luke 12:48.

According to the above quoted Word, God requires some contributions from the rulers of the different nations of the world towards the expansion of His kingdom, by reason of the recognition and high premium He bestows upon them.

God requires the rulers of the world to contribute to the engagement of the instrumentality of the Gospel to tackle the nagging problems ravaging the world.

The problems ravaging the world come from many different angles: human, economic, weather, and many others.

The human angle is about the most virulent of all the angles; as evidenced by the acts of terrorism.

In that connection, I will like to revert to part of the things I wrote in Chapter Five of this book under the title: Way out of Terrorism:

" **'Long-term' Measure: Divine Power Application**

> In view of all that are written so far in this book, it is evident that there is no human governmental power in this world that can finally resolve the issue of terrorism without reverting to the plan of God concerning it.
>
> Any attempt taken, as potent, genuine, and well- meaning as it may be, will only be like a swinging pendulum which at the time of rest comes back to the starting point. You keep on reacting it to make it swing again. The long-term and permanent measure for the peoples of the world is to be on the Lord's side, promoting the expansion of the Kingdom of God which Jesus brought to the world; that is, to imbibe the New Testament Gospel of the Lord Jesus Christ relentlessly.
>
> The peoples of the world need a well- planned input of global campaign for the free flow of the Gospel"

God requires the rulers of the different nations of the world to lead the way in this well- planned input of global campaign for the free flow of the Gospel.

Throughout this book, it is pointed out that terrorism occurs due to lack of understanding of God and His acts by the peoples that engage in terrorism.

That is, the problem of terrorism is a spiritual problem; the problem has the root in the spirit realm.

We cannot effectively eradicate a thing that is outside our control.

We cannot use earthly realm devices to eradicate an evil whose root is in the spirit realm.

The use of earthly realm devices can only produce palliative results rather than curative results. The device which the Kingdom of God provides is the Gospel of peace and love which is enclosed in the programs of the Kingdom of God which Jesus Christ brought to the world.

That is why the use of the earthly realm devices comes under the 'short-term' measure discussed in Chapter Five of this book.

The Kingdom of God in the spirit realm, where Jesus has already taken care of all the things that pertain to the entire human race, is the place where the power that can finally terminate terrorism resides; because terrorism is a spiritual problem.

Also, God's Word says:

> "For unto us a child is born, unto us a son is given: and the government shall be upon his shoulder: and his name shall be called Wonderful, Counselor, The mighty God, The everlasting Father, The Prince of Peace. Of the increase of his government and peace there shall be no end, upon the throne of David, and upon his kingdom, to order it, and to establish it with judgment and with justice from henceforth even for ever. The zeal of the LORD of hosts will perform this." saiah 9:6-7.

The Word just quoted is the prophecy of God concerning the ministry and performance of Jesus Christ upon earth.

The overall governmental affairs of this world are upon the shoulder of Jesus Christ. So, Jesus Christ instructs His believers to obey the rulers, as highlighted earlier.

There shall be no end to the increase of the government of Jesus Christ, and the increase of His peace. That is, there will be unlimited expansion of righteous government and peace upon earth. The Word says good judgment and justice will prevail even forever.

The joy of it all is that the zeal of God -- the commitment of God by His Spirit-- will perform all the above blessings.

That is, the commitment of God will be received when the peoples of the world have taken the steps of faith; and have engaged themselves practically in the promotion of the Kingdom of God.

The unlimited power of God's Spirit, the Holy Spirit, will come into action to get the desired things done. That is why God's Word tells us:

> "Faithful is he that calleth you, who also will do it." --
> -- 1 Thessalonians 5:24.

Meaning that when the peoples take the steps of faith, our faithful and dependable God will back-up the actions of faith taken.

The principle of the Kingdom of God is that in all things that the world requires of God, there must be first a willing mind—2 Corinthians 8:12 on the part of the people to contribute practical works of faith so that the desired thing can be accomplished.

The world does not need to undergo any hassle in eradicating terrorism.

All that the world needs to do is act like Peter (then Simon) did, as recorded in the Word quoted below:

"Now when he had left speaking, he said unto Simon, Launch out into the deep, and let down your nets for a draught. And Simon answering said unto him, Master, we have toiled all the night, and have taken nothing: nevertheless at thy word I will let down the net. And when they had this done, they inclosed a great multitude of fishes: and their net brake."—-Luke 5:4 - 6.

In the above Word of God, all that Simon did was he agreed with Jesus, and did what Jesus told him to do; even though they had toiled all night; and had caught no fish.

Consequently, God's Word in 1 Thessalonians 5:24 quoted above got fulfilled in his life, because God ensured that he caught a great multitude of fishes by doing what Jesus told him to do.

What the world needs is to agree with Jesus by joining hands with Him to promote and propagate His Gospel of peace enclosed in His Words.

The entire human race will be surprised as they discover that the Word of God in
1 Thessalonians 5:24 is fulfilled; as the creative power in the Words of God create peace to replace terrorism.

The scriptures, while projecting the life and ministry of Jesus ahead of time, had prophesied as written:

"Thy throne, O God, is for ever and ever: the sceptre of thy kingdom is a right sceptre. Thou lovest righteousness, and hatest wickedness: therefore God, thy God, hath anointed thee with the oil of gladness above thy fellows." Psalm 45:6 - 7.

His anointed life and ministry are parts of the great virtues Jesus had brought to join the entire world together as one peaceful environment.

God's Word in Hebrews 1:3 says God upholds all things by the Word of His power.

The various God's Words have been highlighted, which will eliminate terrorism if the world will do what the Words say.

Doing what the Words say will start by accepting Jesus; and joining Him in the works of the expansion of the Kingdom of God.

It is Up to the World

It is up to the world to decide whether to "halt between two opinions" (1 Kings 18:21}; whether to receive Jesus towards the termination of terrorism, or whether to succumb to the whims and caprices of the terrorists.

Right now, the world concentrates mainly on fighting against the terrorists.

The world does not concentrate on the acceptance of Jesus; whereas, terrorism originated inadvertently from the family of Abraham; and whereas, Jesus, the Son of God, came to the world in the flesh-- as a human being-- through the loins of Abraham, bringing the Kingdom of God to the world, part of which purpose is to bring terrorism to an end.

The present situation in the world stands as a clarion call on the entire world to stand up and receive Jesus Christ.

Therefore, as the world searches for the means to stop terrorism, I pray the Word of God will be speedily fulfilled in the lives of the entire human race, as written:

"And ye shall seek me, and find me, when ye shall search for me with all your heart."

-----Jeremiah 29:13.

I pray the whole world will yield to God through Jesus Christ.

I pray some peoples of the world will desist from using God-given talents to produce weapons for the destruction of lives and properties; that the talents will be used to produce equipment to sustain the abundant life— spiritually, physically, and materially-- for which Jesus came to the world (John 10:10) – that the equipment will cater for the peoples' physical, medical, and material needs.

Do the peoples of the world not realize that the knowledge exhibited by all physical, chemical, biological, medical, and several other scientists in all the nations of the world are gifts bestowed on these scientists as endowments from God for the benefits of all humanity? ------ Proverbs 8:12; Proverbs 8:31; James 1:17.

I pray the whole world will obey the Word of God which says: "Seek peace, and pursue it" (Psalm 34:14).

In Jesus' name I have prayed. Amen.

Chapter seven

God's Endowments Start with Salvation

God's endowments upon a person are great gifts from God. Speaking by the Spirit, Apostle Paul admonished Timothy, as written:

"Wherefore I put thee in remembrance that thou stir up the gift of God, which is in thee by the putting on of my hands." -—2 Timothy 1:6

Every gift of God has life; therefore, it can grow. And for the gift to grow, it must be stirred up, as stated in the above quoted Word.

The Word of God in the Bible is the stirring rod for stirring up every gift of God; otherwise, the gift becomes dead and redundant.

Getting the profitable stirring rod, that is, the Word of God, starts by getting the salvation of the Lord Jesus Christ.

Getting the salvation of Jesus starts by going through God's recommended process.

In case you have not received Jesus into your life, you are enjoined to go through God's recommended process of salvation by saying the following things:

"Lord Jesus, I come to You today. I am a sinner. I repent of my sins. I believe in my heart that You are the Son of the Living God. I believe that You came to this world to save sinners. Forgive me of my sins. Save me. I confess You as my Lord and Savior. Wash me clean with Your shed blood. Put the Holy Spirit in me as a seal of my salvation. I turn my back on Satan to serve the Living God. Thank You Jesus for saving me. I am born again."

God's Word says:

"For with the heart man believeth unto righteousness; and with the mouth confession is made unto salvation." Romans 10:10

Having believed Jesus with your heart and having confessed Him with your mouth, Jesus has given you salvation, and has received you into the realm of righteousness with God.

The endowments of God shall be bestowed upon you as you fellowship with Jesus and with the brothers and sisters in church services, Christian fellowship gatherings, by continuously reading your Bible, and by engaging yourself in acts that promote the Kingdom of God, as written:

"But seek ye first the kingdom of God, and his righteousness; and all these things shall be added unto you." Matthew 6:33.

By engaging in acts that promote the expansion of the Kingdom of God, you shall receive continuous and higher infillings of the Holy Spirit.

The Holy Spirit will continuously empower you to receive increased levels of God's endowments.

I pray all that are written above shall be your experience, your testimony and your song. In Jesus' name. Amen.

ADDENDUM

GOD'S PROJECTED CONVERGENCE OF ISAAC AND ISHMAEL

Even though God was not pleased with the plan whereby Sarai gave Hagar to Abraham to be his wife, God gave the name Ishmael to Hagar's son as written:

> "And the angel of the LORD said unto her, Behold, thou art with child, and shalt bear a son, and shalt call his name Ishmael; because the LORD hath heard thy affliction."

> -------Genesis 16:11.

Also, Sarah, Abraham's legitimate wife, had a son at God's own time; and God gave the name Isaac to Sarah's son. God also accorded recognition to Isaac and Ishmael in different ways as written:

> "And Abraham said unto God, O that Ishmael might live before thee! And God said, Sarah thy wife shall bear thee a son indeed; and thou shalt call his name Isaac: and I will establish my covenant with him for an everlasting covenant, and with his seed after him. And as for Ishmael, I have heart thee: Behold, I have blessed him, and will make him fruitful, and will multiply him exceedingly; twelve princes shall he beget, and I will make him a great nation. But my covenant will I establish with Isaac, which Sarah shall bear unto thee at this set time next year." Genesis 17:18 - 21.

The assignment of the names of Ishmael and Isaac by God was in pursuance of a projected plan to converge Ishmael and Isaac together in Jesus Christ.

Also, the answer God gave to Abraham concerning his petition to God about Ishmael is highly delightful:

'And as for Ishmael, I have heard thee' Genesis 17:20

When you make your petition to God, and you know He has heard you, then you are in for a break-through into great things which are ahead of you!

So, terrorism had been forestalled right from the beginnings of Ishmael's and Isaac's lives journeys on earth.

The forestallment of terrorism is more assured because as stated earlier in this book, the description of Ishmael by the angel of God was made in hope, as written:

> "For the earnest expectation of the creature waiteh for the manifestation of the sons of God. For the creature was made subject to vanity, not willingly, but by reason of him who hath subjected the same in hope, Because the creature itself also shall be delivered from the bondage of corruption into the glorious liberty of the children of God."

------Romans 8:19 - 21

As explained earlier in this book, the description of Ishmael by the angel of God was made in hope of better times when God's original intention for the world would have been restored— when there shall be no terrorism in the world because the Kingdom of God relates to the whole world without any exception.

And Jesus came to fulfill that hope over two thousand years ago. <u>God's Projected Plan and Purpose for the World</u>

God's projected plan and purpose for the peoples of the world is spiritual in content and in power because it is an incident from above.

God's projected plan and purpose for the peoples of the world is routed through God's Son, Jesus Christ.

One of the several God's Words towards that intent says:

> "For God so loved the world, that he gave his only begotten Son, that whosoever believeth in him should not perish, but have everlasting life. For God sent not his Son into the world to condemn the world; but that the world through him might be saved."

-------John 3:16 - 17

Jesus came to the world over two thousand years ago to fulfill the plan and purpose of God for the peoples of the world.

Concerning this assignment of Jesus, the Bible records as follows:

> "For he whom God hath sent speaketh the words of God: for God giveth not the Spirit by measure unto him. The Father loveth the Son, and hath given all things into his hand. He that believeth on the Son hath everlasting life: and he that believeth not the Son shall not see life; but the wrath of God abideth on him." John 3:34 - 36

Jesus Christ is the Son of God whom God had sent to the world to carry out God's assignments. Jesus Christ came in the flesh---as a human being—; but God the Father gave the Holy Spirit to Him in full, not by measure to do His assignments.

And having completed all His assignments on the earth, the Bible records the ascension of Jesus into heaven after speaking unto His disciples, as written:

"So then after the Lord had spoken unto them, he was received up into heaven, and sat on the right hand of God." Mark 16:19

Right now, Jesus Christ is seated on the right hand of God on the throne of God in heaven; while born again Christians await His second coming.

<u>In summary:</u>
The summary of all that are written so far under this section is that the description of Ishmael was made from heaven in hope of the convergence of Ishmael and Isaac through the ministry of Jesus Christ upon earth.

Let all the generational descendants of Ishmael and all the generational descendants of Isaac focus on the acceptance of Jesus Christ.

THE KINGDOM OF GOD BELONGS TO GOD

THE KINGDOM OF GOD DOES NOT BELONG TO ANY HUMAN BEING

Under the preceding title: GOD'S PROJECTED CONVERGENCE OF ISAAC AND ISHMAEL, it is stated that the Kingdom of God relates to the whole world without any exception.

To be specific, the Kingdom of God belongs to God.

The Kingdom of God does not belong to any human being.

The Kingdom of God does not belong to the generational descendants of Isaac. The Kingdom of God does not belong to the generational descendants of Ishmael.

The Kingdom of God, which belongs to God, was brought to the world by Jesus Christ, the Son of God.

The Kingdom of God was brought to the world for administration on behalf of the peoples of the world, as detailed below:

When Jesus was going away, He told His disciples:

"But now I go my way to him that sent me; and none of you asketh me, Wither goest thou? But because I have said these things unto you, sorrow hath filled your heart. Nevertheless I tell you the truth; It is expedient for you that I go away: for if I go not away, the Comforter will not come unto you; but if I depart, I will send him unto you. I have yet many things to say unto you, but ye cannot bear them now. Howbeit when he, the Spirit of truth, is come, he will guide you into all truth: for he shall not speak of himself; but whatsoever he shall hear, that shall he speak: and he will shew you things to come. He shall glorify me: for he shall receive of mine, and shew it unto you. "

------John 16:5 - 7; 12 - 14

In the above quoted Word, Jesus Christ promised to send the Comforter, the Holy Spirit, after He would have gone away.

As a fulfilment of the promise of Jesus Christ, the Holy Spirit came to earth on the day of Pentecost, as written:

"And when the day of Pentecost was fully come, they were all with one accord in one place. And suddenly there came a sound from heaven as of a rushing mighty wind, and it filled all the house where they were sitting. And there appeared unto them cloven tongues like as of fire, and it sat upon each of them. And they were all filled with the Holy Ghost, and began to speak with other tongues, as the Spirit gave them utterance."

--------Acts 2:1 - 4

The Holy Spirit, Who came to the earth on the day of Pentecost, had been resident in the earth up till now.

<u>Administration of the Kingdom of God</u>

The Holy Spirit is the Administrator of the Kingdom of God.

The Holy Spirit administers the Kingdom of God to glorify Jesus (John 16:14) for the expansion of the Kingdom.

Whatever practices or behaviors that do not glorify Jesus must be put away when any person comes to the Kingdom of God; as entrance into the Kingdom of God can be embarked upon only through Jesus Christ.

The Kingdom of God is loaded with uncountable benefits for the whole world.

Every inhabitant of the world, no matter his or her location, no matter his or her inclination, is free to come to Jesus, worship God in spirit and in truth through Jesus Christ (John 4:23 - 24); and partake of the Kingdom of God.

In other words, any person in the world who desires to partake of the benefits of the Kingdom of God must come to God through Jesus Christ.

Jesus says:

"I am the way, the truth, and the life: no man cometh unto the Father, but by me."

-----John 14:6

And Jesus further says:

"All things are delivered unto me of my Father: and no man knoweth the Son, but the Father; neither knoweth any man the Father, save the Son, and he to whomsoever the Son will reveal him. Come unto me, all ye that labour and are heavy laden, and I will give you rest. Take my yoke upon you, and learn of me; for I am meek and lowly in heart: and ye shall find rest unto your souls. For my yoke is easy, and my burden is light."

------Matthew 11:27 - 30

The Bible gives the following testimony concerning all the peoples that have accepted Jesus Christ, and worship God in spirit and in truth through Jesus Christ:

"Blessed be the God and Father of our Lord Jesus Christ, who hath blessed us with all spiritual blessings in heavenly places in Christ: According as he hath chosen us in him before the foundation of the world, that we should be holy and without blame before him in love: Having predestinated us unto the adoption of children by Jesus Christ to himself, according to the good pleasure of his will, To the praise of the glory of his grace, wherein he hath made us accepted in the beloved." Ephesians 1:3 - 6

Jesus is calling on the entire members of the generational descendants of Ishmael and the entire members of the generational descendants of Isaac to come to the Kingdom of God through Him; and worship God in spirit and in truth through Him.

That is the plan of God for His Kingdom in the world that terrorism may come to an end.

EMBARK ON YOUR JOURNEY TO THE KINGDOM OF GOD

THE REASON GOD CREATED THE WORLD

The Bible says:

"And the LORD God planted a garden eastward in Eden; and there he put the man whom he had formed. And out of the ground made the LORD God to grow every tree that is pleasant to the sight, and good for food; the tree of life also in the midst of the garden, and the tree of knowledge of good and evil." Genesis 2:8 - 9.

"And the LORD God commanded the man, saying, Of every tree of the garden thou mayest freely eat: But of the tree of the knowledge of good and evil, thou shalt not eat of it: for in the day that thou eatest thereof thou shalt surely die." Genesis 2:16 - 17.

"Now the serpent was more subtil than any beast of the field which the LORD God had made. And he said unto the woman, Yea, hath God said, Ye shall not eat of every tree of the garden? And the woman said unto the serpent, We may eat of the fruit of the trees of the garden: But the fruit of the tree which is in the midst of the garden, God hath said, Ye shall not eat of it, neither shall ye touch it, lest ye die. And the serpent said unto the woman, Ye shall not surely die: For God doth know that in the day ye eat thereof, then your eyes shall be opened, and ye shall be as Gods, knowing good and evil. And when the woman saw that the tree was good for food, and that it was pleasant to the eyes, and a tree to be desired to make one wise, she took of the fruit thereof, and did eat, and gave also unto her husband with her; and he did eat." Genesis 3:1 - 6.

God created the world so He could bring His kingdom to the world.

Towards that end, God created Adam and Eve, and God commanded them to eat the tree of life which was in the garden of Eden Genesis 2:8 - 9; Genesis 2:16 - 17.

However, Adam and Eve were deceived by serpent the devil to eat the fruit of the tree of the knowledge of good and evil.

So, Adam and Eve disobeyed the commandment God gave them in Genesis 2:16 - 17. Consequently, Adam and Eve died a spiritual death, as God had told them.

Also, Adam and Eve were chased out of the garden of Eden, the garden that contained all that a person needs for life fulfilment, into the world of vanity, frustration, and hopelessness.

Therefore, everyone born into this world is born into spiritual death, vanity, frustration, and hopelessness.

The Advent of Jesus Christ

Jesus, the Son of God, came to the world.

Jesus came as a human being through the loins of Abraham, according to the will of God the Father.

Jesus brought the Kingdom of God to the world, a task which Adam failed to accomplish. Jesus came to quicken every person that accepts Him out of the spiritual death; and to deliver that person from vanity, insecurity, and hopelessness.

Consequently, concerning Jesus, the Bible says:

"And so it is written, The first man Adam was made a living soul; the last Adam was made a quickening spirit."
1 Corinthians 15:45.

Jesus was the last Adam, the quickening Spirit. Jesus brought grace and truth, as written:

"For the law was given by Moses, but grace and truth came by Jesus Christ."
----John 1:17

The tree of life which God commanded Adam and Eve to eat in Genesis 2:8 - 9, and in Genesis 2:16 - 17, symbolized the grace and truth which Jesus brought in John 1:17.

Also, Romans 8:2 says:

"For the law of the Spirit of life in Christ Jesus hath made me free from the law of sin and death." Romans 8:2

The tree of life which God commanded Adam and Eve to eat in Genesis 2:8 - 9, and in Genesis 2:16 - 17, symbolized the Spirit of life in Romans 8:2.

The tree of life also symbolized freedom from the law of sin and death in Romans 8:2

Summarily, Jesus brought all the things human beings need for life fulfilment, as provided in the garden of Eden.

Again, Jesus brought grace and truth, as written:

"For the law was given by Moses, but grace and truth came by Jesus Christ."
----John 1:17

God said Adam and Eve should not eat the tree of the knowledge of good and evil. This tree of the knowledge of good and evil puts a person under the law John 1:17.

This tree of the knowledge of good and evil robs a person of the Spirit of life which is in Christ Jesus ---Romans 8:2.

This tree of the knowledge of good and evil puts a person under the law of sin and death ---Romans 8:2.

In other words, God wanted Adam and Eve to be under grace and truth; God did not want them to be under the law John 1:17.

Unfortunately, Adam and Eve disobeyed this commandment of God due to Satan's deception. By that disobedience, Adam and Eve brought themselves out of grace and truth; and put themselves under the law of sin and death.

And by that, every born person is born into the law of sin and death.

Jesus came to the world to take human beings away from under the law; and bring them back to under grace and truth which was the original plan of God for human beings when He created the world. That is the plan of God for the operation of His Kingdom.

Come to Jesus today, and be a partaker of the Kingdom of God, no matter wherever your location is in the world. No matter whatever your inclination is right now, get redeemed unto God by Jesus Christ.

WORLD'S RECURRENT DANGERS OF REFUSING TO ACCEPT JESUS CHRIST

Point of Reference:

The Angel's Contrary Word to Hagar about Ishmael

The Word of the angel of the Lord to Hagar concerning Ishmael is as written:

"And the angel of the LORD found her by a fountain of water in the wilderness, by the fountain in the way to Shur. And he said, Hagar, Sarai's maid, whence camest thou? and wither wilt thou go? And she said, I flee from the face of my mistress Sarai. And the angel of the LORD said unto her, Return unto thy mistress, and submit thyself under her hands. And the angel of the LORD said unto her, I will multiply thy seed exceedingly, that it shall not be numbered for multitude. And the angel of the LORD said unto her, Behold, thou art with child, and shalt bear a son, and shalt call his name Ishmael; because the LORD hath heard thy affliction. And he will be a wild man; his hand will be against every man, and every man's hand against him; and he shall dwell in the presence of all his brethren." Genesis 16: 7 - 12.

The contrary Word which the angel of the LORD pronounced on Ishmael depicted an attitude that engenders terrorism and counter terrorism—a situation that results in severe consequences, and severe discomfort on every side concerned.

Because the act of terror will always involve two sides of human beings - the giver of the infliction of terror, and the receiver of the infliction of terror.

The two sides involved are the generational descendants of Ishmael and the generational descendants of Isaac.

Also, the contrary Word of the angel of the LORD concerning Ishmael builds a foundation of a bloody confrontational spirit into Ishmael and his generational descendants. How?

The answer and the explanation concerning 'how' is as follows:

When Adam sinned by eating the forbidden--fruit he died a spiritual death as God had told him. Consequently, every person born into this world is born into sin and spiritual death; and only the salvation of the Lord Jesus Christ can deliver that person from the sin and spiritual death.

The Bible summarizes this incident, as written:

> "For all have sinned, and come short of the glory of God; Being justified freely by his grace through the redemption that is in Christ Jesus:" Romans 3:23--24

Likewise, any contrary Word from God to any person before the time Jesus came to the world, will reflect on the generational descendants of that person until the generational descendants come to Jesus to receive salvation and deliverance. Because Jesus came to take care of all the peoples of the world, no matter the circumstances surrounding any people.

<u>Bloody Confrontational Tendency Cancelled</u>

Jesus had taken care of that bloody confrontational spirit, nailed it to His cross, and blotted it out of any person that accepts Him.

So, any person or any group of people should not manifest that bloody confrontational spirit anymore, by displaying it under any guise: either openly or under cover, or in an implied manner, or in any way akin to it.

But that will depend on that person or group of people accepting Jesus Christ; and worshipping God in spirit and in truth through Jesus Christ.

Jesus will not want any individual or any established authority to manifest the bloody confrontational spirit, whether from the peoples among the generational descendants of Ishmael, or from the peoples among the generational descendants of Isaac.

Jesus forbids the act of engaging in any human law that inflicts terror, discomfort, and fear on the people, whether from the generational descendants of Ishmael, or from the generational descendants of Isaac: because that act amounts to terrorism in disguised shade.

Jesus is not alone in the assignment He came to do in the world. Jesus says:

> "And he that sent me is with me: the Father hath not left me alone; for I do always those things that please him." John 8:29

The implication of all that are written so far is as follows:

In so much as the world refuses to accept Jesus Christ, the world will continue to grapple with terrorism.

God will not bend or break His Words to suit the world. It is the world that will bend and adjust to God's Words.

Do we not know that all human actions and deeds in the earthly realm have the control roots in the spirit realm--where both the forces of the good and the forces of the evil abide—so that the forces of the evil corrupt God's Words and plans in the minds of the peoples?

Do not allow the devil to control your mind. Yield your mind to God through Jesus Christ. Jesus is Lord.

Concerning Jesus Christ, the following is written:

"Wherefore he is able also to save them to the uttermost that come unto God by him, seeing he ever liveth to make intercession for them." Hebrews 7:25

Jesus is the Savior of the world. Come to Jesus today.

Worship God in spirit and in truth through Jesus Christ. Contribute to the end of terrorism in the world.

ABOUT THE AUTHOR

Moses Talabi, became a born- again Christian in July 1991 at the age of 56.

He is the founder of Jesus' Legacies Ministry International Inc. (JLMI), a United States nonprofit ministry.

He has passion for printed evangelism; especially the inherent power and intents of the Words of God as they relate to the New Testament, New Covenant life and experiences in the Kingdom of God which Jesus brought to the world.

The printed evangelism is done under the auspices of Jesus' Legacies Publishers, a division of JLMI.

Moses Talabi, is married to Funke; with off springs. Moses Talabi, is the author of:

The Mystery of Your Relationship with Christ The Christian Law of Righteousness

You Are Elected Coordinator of God's Business

THIS PAGE WAS INTENTIONALLY LEFT BLANK